ADVENTURE GIRLS!

ADVENTURE GIRLS!

CRAFTS AND ACTIVITIES FOR
CURIOUS, CREATIVE, COURAGEOUS GIRLS

NICOLE DUGGAN

ILLUSTRATED BY CAIT BRENNAN

ROCKRIDGE
PRESS

For general information on our other products and services or to obtain technical support, please contact our Customer Care Department within the United States at (866) 744-2665, or outside the United States at (510) 253-0500.

Rockridge Press publishes its books in a variety of electronic and print formats. Some content that appears in print may not be available in electronic books, and vice versa.

Interior and Cover Designer: Tricia Jang
Art Producer: Sue Bischofberger
Editor: Mary Colgan
Production Manager: Oriana Siska
Production Editor: Melissa Edeburn

Illustration © 2019 Cait Brennan

ISBN: Print 978-1-64152-742-2
eBook 978-1-64152-743-9

To my daughter, **Natalie**,
who is always up for an adventure,
and to my son, **Blake**,
who loves a challenge.

CONTENTS

Introduction 1

Finding Your Way 2

Nature Scavenger Hunt 10

Hit the Trail 16

Wind and Weather 20

Animal Tracks 30

A Photographer's Eye 36

Tying Knots 40

A Backyard Hideaway 46

Stargazing 50

Down in the Dirt 56

Bird Watching 62

Make It Float 70

Neighborhood Games 74

Shadow Theater 80

Spice It Up 84

Paper Airplanes 88

Make Your Own Board Game 94

Clown Around 96

Fun with Flowers 102

Origami 106

Cracking the Code 114

Bookworms 120

Playing in Trees 122

Practice Kindness 126

10 More Adventurous Women Through History 128

INTRODUCTION

I wrote this book for you, *ADVENTURE GIRL*, to give you ideas and inspiration to try new things.

In this book you will discover information about animals, plants, constellations, and maps, as well as ways to entertain people with magic tricks, shadow puppets, and balloon animals. You will be introduced to origami, knot tying, photography, and much more. My goal is for you to experience something new that sparks your curiosity.

There are many remarkable women featured in this book who have achieved incredible things while showing courage and determination. I hope their stories inspire you to dream big and never give up.

My hope is that this book will encourage you to explore nature, your community, and the world around you, and to spread kindness as you go.

BE BRAVE, BE ADVENTUROUS, BE CREATIVE, AND—MOST IMPORTANTLY—BE YOU!

FINDING YOUR WAY

Being able to figure out where you are and where you are headed is an important skill, especially for Adventure Girls who are always on the go. There are many important tools that can help you find your way.

HOW TO READ A MAP

Reading a map can seem tricky at first, but there are two things that will help you: the legend and the compass rose.

THE LEGEND is a chart with symbols that represent different things on the map. There might be black lines for roads and blue lines for rivers, dots for cities, and squares that represent houses or restaurants. Different types of maps have different symbols, but they are all found in the legend.

compass rose

A COMPASS ROSE shows direction on the map: north, east, south, and west. To remember the order of the directions you can always remember the saying "Never Eat Shredded Wheat" (North, East, South, West). Or, if you know that north is at the top, the middle of the compass rose always spells "WE" (West, East).

Sometimes figuring out where you are on the map is the hardest part. If you are looking at a map and trying to find where you are located, look for two streets that cross near you that you can also find on the map. Are there any landmarks or places near you that you can identify on the map to help figure out where you are? If you have a compass (see page 6 to learn how to make your own), you can also determine which way is north and turn the map so the top is facing that direction.

As you continue, pay attention to roads or landmarks that you are passing to help you figure out which way you are moving on the map.

LOOK TO THE SKY

Even without a map, Adventure Girls can find their way by studying the sky. Day or night, there is a lot you can figure out just by using your eyes, your mind, and some simple steps.

USE THE SUN

1   Push a straight medium-sized stick into the ground so it's upright.

2   Put a rock at the end of its shadow.

3   Wait about 15 minutes and the shadow will have moved. Put another rock at the end of where the shadow is now.

4   Take your stick out of the ground and lay it down between the two rocks.

5   The stick will be pointing north and south. The first rock you put down represents west, and the second rock is east. The sticks and rocks represent a compass rose.

USE THE STARS

You can also use stars in the night sky to find direction. One constellation that is easy to find is called Orion, which is most visible from November through February. You will see three very bright stars in a straight line: That is called Orion's Belt. If you look under the third star of Orion's belt, you will see two more stars in a line going down. Those three stars form Orion's Sword. Orion's Sword always points to the south. If you see Orion's Sword in the night sky, you can move in that direction and know that you are heading south.

SEA TURTLES

Did you know that sea turtles always make their way back to where they were born to lay their eggs? How do they remember their way? Just like we use the compass rose on a map, sea turtles use Earth's magnetic field to find their way. The earth is filled with iron, which has a magnetic field around it. Earth's magnetic field points north. Sea turtles use the magnetic field to find their way back home.

MAKE YOUR OWN COMPASS

With a compass to tell you which direction you are headed, you will never get lost! You can buy a compass to keep with you during outdoor adventures, but you can also make your own compass to experiment with how it works.

WHAT YOU'LL NEED

Metal needle (ask a parent's permission first)

Magnet

Tape

Piece of Styrofoam or cork (something light that can float)

Water

Small bowl

Paper

Pencil or marker

1 Rub the needle with a magnet, from the bottom of the needle to the top, about 15 times. Don't rub back and forth; always rub from the bottom to the top. Once you have done that, the needle is magnetized.

2 Tape the needle on a small piece of Styrofoam or cork. If you don't have Styrofoam or cork, find something else that is lightweight and can float.

3 Drop the Styrofoam and needle into the water. Watch the needle turn! It will point north.

4 Write "North," "East," "South," and "West" on small pieces of paper. Tape "North" in front of the point of the needle and the others around the bowl like a compass rose.

5 You can use another compass if you have one or use the sun (page 4) to see that your compass works.

6 Even if you turn the bowl or take out the needle and drop it back in the water again and again, it will always turn and point to the north. The magnetized needle is drawn to Earth's magnetic north.

MAKE YOUR OWN MAP

Adventure Girls can read maps, but they can also create their own maps! Put your map skills and creativity to the test to make a map that is both a useful tool and a piece of art.

WHAT YOU'LL NEED

Paper

Markers or crayons

1 Decide what location you are going to draw as a map. You could choose any place familiar to you: your bedroom, yard, neighborhood, school, park, or local grocery store.

2 Draw the outline or shape of your space. It won't always be a square. Look closely at the edges of the area you are drawing and make your map the same shape.

3 Draw the details of your space, starting with the biggest items. This is a great time to add a legend. You can use squares for houses or desks, lines for roads or trees, and circles to represent tables or cars. Make sure to include the shape and the color in your legend.

4 Pay attention to how close or far apart things are in your space. Are they on opposite walls? Next to each other? Does your map match?

5 Once your map has the details that you want, challenge someone else to read your map and see if they can use the legend to identify what different symbols stand for. You could even hide a treasure and mark it on your map for someone to find.

> **⋛ FUN TIP ⋚**
> Create maps of all your favorite places and put them together as an atlas of all the important places in your life.

ADVENTURE GIRL CHALLENGE

Next time you are in a place where a map is available, volunteer to be in charge of reading the map for your group. You can find maps on hiking trails, at the zoo, in amusement parks, or on the train.

NATURE SCAVENGER HUNT

There are so many things to see and discover in nature. From different rocks and leaves to insects and animals, nature is full of colorful treasures waiting to be found.

THE HUNT

Let's go on a scavenger hunt, Adventure Girl! Collect these items in a T-shirt bag (page 12), take pictures of them, or just check them off the list when you find them. Go on this hunt over and over again and challenge yourself to find new things.

> **⋛ FUN TIP ⋚**
> Make a collage out of things you collected on your hunt.

2 different shaped leaves
special rock
animal tracks
piece of bark
stick
something tall
something small
something noisy
something that moves
something living
something that grows
something sharp
something smooth
something rough
something fuzzy
something with a scent
something colorful

MAKE A T-SHIRT TREASURE BAG

Turn an old T-shirt into a bag to collect your treasures and discoveries. You can also use your bag when you shop to avoid using plastic bags.

WHAT YOU'LL NEED

Old T-shirt

Scissors

Ruler

Marker

1 Turn a T-shirt inside out and lay it flat on the table. Any size T-shirt will work, but the bigger the shirt, the bigger the bag you will make.

2 Cut off each sleeve.

3 Cut off the collar, using the seam to guide you and make it even.

4 Use a ruler to draw a line across the shirt about 5 inches from the bottom.

5 Starting at the bottom of the shirt, cut strips about 1-inch wide through both layers to make a fringe. Don't cut past the line you drew and make sure both sides match.

STEPS 2 & 3

STEP 5

6 Take the first pair of fringes and tie them together in a knot. Continue along the bottom until each pair is tied in a knot.

7 Turn the shirt right side out so that the tied fringe is on the inside.

STEP 6

MAKE A NATURE BOWL

Turn things you've found in nature into a unique bowl. You can keep it in your room to hold treasures that you find on your outdoor adventures.

WHAT YOU'LL NEED

Natural items such as leaves, grass, and flowers

Balloon

Medium bowl

White glue

Water

Paintbrush

Scissors

1 Collect natural items from your yard, neighborhood, or on your next hike.

2 Blow up and tie a balloon.

3 Put the bottom half of the balloon in a bowl to keep it steady while you work.

4 Mix together equal parts glue and water.

5 Paint the glue mixture onto half of the balloon.

6 Stick leaves or flowers onto the balloon where you have painted the glue mixture.

7 Keep adding glue and more leaves and flowers so that they overlap and completely cover the top half of the balloon. You can use a lot of glue. It will all dry clear and make the bowl firmer.

8 Let it dry for several hours.

9 Use scissors to pop the balloon.

10 Carefully remove the balloon from the bowl.

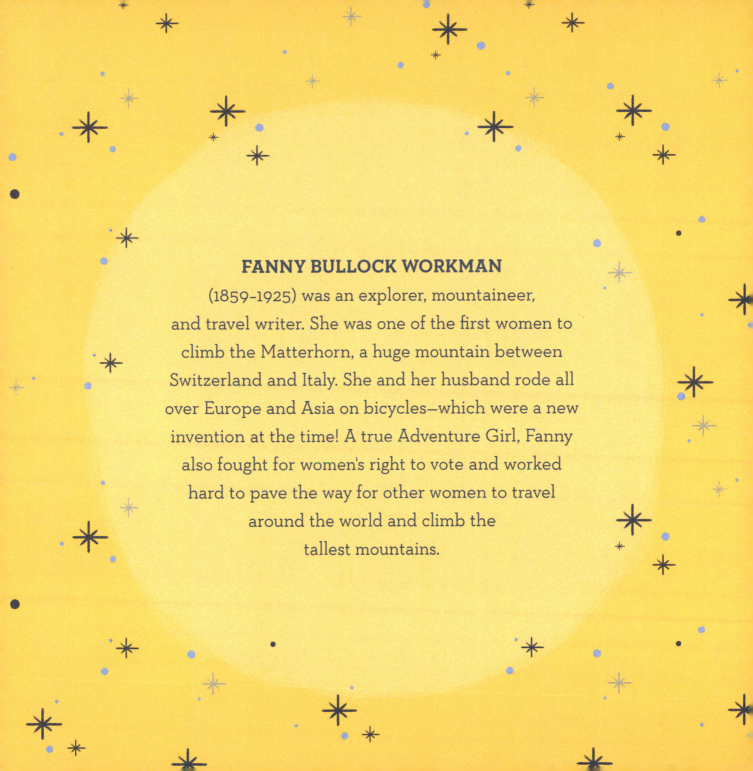

FANNY BULLOCK WORKMAN

(1859-1925) was an explorer, mountaineer, and travel writer. She was one of the first women to climb the Matterhorn, a huge mountain between Switzerland and Italy. She and her husband rode all over Europe and Asia on bicycles—which were a new invention at the time! A true Adventure Girl, Fanny also fought for women's right to vote and worked hard to pave the way for other women to travel around the world and climb the tallest mountains.

HIT THE TRAIL

Hiking is good exercise, but you can also see, hear, and learn so many different things while you walk outdoors. Whether you enjoy quick walks or long hikes, there are many tips and skills for you to use.

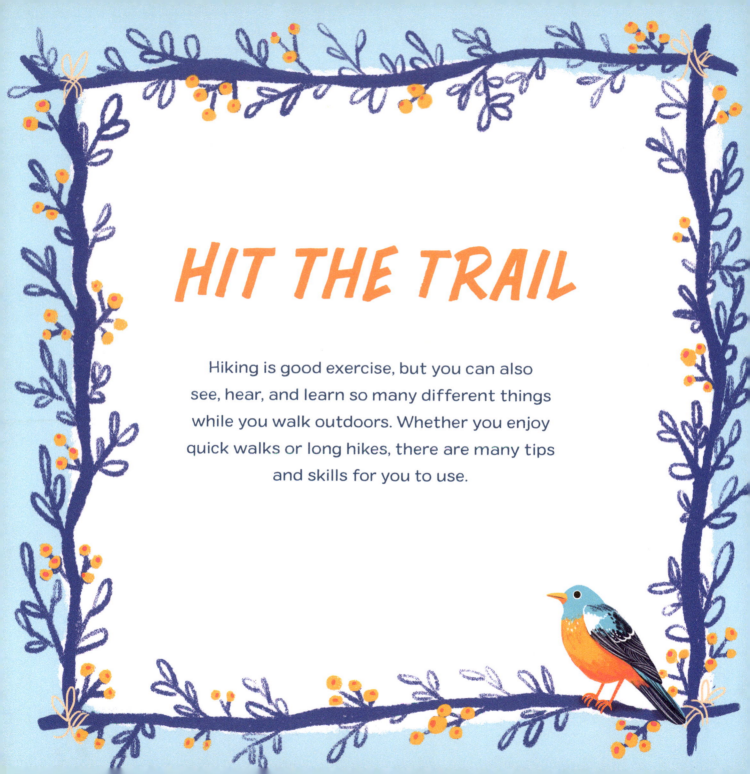

TURN LEFT

STRAIGHT AHEAD

TURN RIGHT

DO NOT GO THIS WAY

I HAVE GONE HOME

TRAIL MARKERS

Trail markers are a way to use natural things to communicate with yourself and others. You can use rocks or sticks to create trail markers. Trail markers can tell someone to go straight, turn right or left, not to go a certain way, or even that you've gone home. Whether you are reminding yourself how to get home or communicating with others about where to go, trail markers are simple to set up and, with practice, easy to read.

> **≽ FUN TIP ≼** Use trail markers for a treasure hunt!

TAKE A CITY HIKE

If you live in or are visiting a city, you can still enjoy a hike. You can walk to a museum, park, school, or garden. Keep an eye out for natural things around you even on the city streets, such as flowers, plants, birds, nests, insects, or spider webs.

WHAT YOU NEED FOR A LONG HIKE

Adventure Girls should always be prepared. To prepare for a long hike, make sure you are wearing the right clothes and shoes. Apply and pack sunscreen and bug spray. Don't forget a map (if there is one) and a compass. Make sure to have water and snacks (like a homemade trail mix), and pack a whistle so that you can use it if you get separated from your group.

MAKE YOUR OWN TRAIL MIX

The best trail mixes include something sweet like chocolate or candy, something crunchy like pretzels or cereal, something healthy like fruit or berries, and something with protein like nuts or seeds. Try mixing chocolate chips, pretzel sticks, raisins, almonds, and sunflower seeds for a tasty, energy-boosting snack. Or invent your own recipe!

NATURE'S PAINTBRUSH

Use things you've collected on your hike to make natural paintbrushes. Experiment with your brushes to find out which are best for painting and other art projects.

WHAT YOU'LL NEED

Natural materials from a hike

Sticks or clothespins

Rubber bands (optional)

Paint and paper (optional)

1 Collect items from your hike such as leaves, flowers, grass, sticks, and bark.

2 Clip each item in a clothespin or use a rubber band to attach each natural item to the end of a stick.

3 Experiment with your new paintbrushes. Dip them in paint and try them on paper, or use water to test them on cement. How does each paintbrush work differently? Which one works the best? Which one can you make better?

ADVENTURE GIRL CHALLENGE

When you get home from your hike, try to draw a map of where you have been from your memory. Include important things you saw along the way like buildings, rivers, fallen trees, or even animal tracks.

WIND AND WEATHER

Whether there's a bright, blue sky or dark, stormy clouds, Adventure Girls can learn, explore, and have fun in any kind of weather. And cool, windy days are a perfect time for weather experiments and playing outdoors. Bundle up and head outside!

PREDICT THE WEATHER

Just like ancient mariners, Adventure Girls can predict the weather by paying attention to the world around them.

FEEL THE WIND

Imagine the wind carrying the temperature and climate from where it is blowing. If the wind is blowing to your area from the south, it will bring warmer and more humid weather. If it is blowing to your area from the north, it will bring cooler and dryer weather. If the wind suddenly changes direction, it could mean a thunderstorm is on the way.

NOTICE HUMIDITY

Humidity is the amount of water in the air. If humidity is high, there is more water in the air and a higher chance that it could rain.

WATCH THE CLOUDS

Clouds give us a lot of help predicting the weather. If there aren't any clouds in the sky or if the clouds are white and fluffy like cotton balls, you can expect good weather.

If you see gray clouds or low clouds, you should prepare for rain that day. Can you see through the clouds? If you can see the sun or the moon through the clouds, then good weather can be expected. If the clouds are thick and you can't see through them, there is a chance for poor weather in the next day or two. If the wind is blowing these clouds in quickly, then the poor weather will arrive faster.

OBSERVE ANIMALS

Scientists have found that animals can sense when the weather is about to turn and change their behavior in response. Frogs, birds, cows, sheep, and even bees have all shown interesting behaviors that are a clue that the weather is changing.

You may hear the sound of frogs become louder and longer, which could mean a storm is coming. Birds fly high in the sky when the weather is good, but if the birds are flying lower, it is because there is bad weather coming. Cows sometimes become restless or lay down before it starts to rain. When sheep start to gather together in a group, it means they are getting ready for a storm. If you see bees or butterflies one day but they're gone the next, rain is probably on the way.

USE A PINECONE

Pinecones give us clues about the moisture in the air. The cone scales close up in damp or rainy weather. When the weather is dry, the pinecone's scales will open back up. Next time you see a pinecone, look at it for clues about the weather.

ADVENTURE GIRL CHALLENGE

Use what you've learned to predict something about the weather each day for a week. Is it going to be rainy, windy, or sunny? Out of seven days, how many did you predict correctly?

MAKE A WEATHER VANE

A weather vane helps you see which direction the wind is blowing. You usually see them on top of buildings or barns. You can make a simple weather vane to learn more about wind and weather.

WHAT YOU'LL NEED

Cardboard or card stock

Scissors

Drinking straw

Straight pin (used in sewing)

Pencil with an eraser

Play dough or a small container filled with sand or soil

Paper plate

Pen

1 Cut a triangle and a square out of a piece of cardboard or card stock. Make sure the square is bigger than the triangle.

2 Using scissors, cut a 1-inch (or smaller) slit at the top and bottom of each end of the straw.

3 Slide the triangle into the slits at one end of the straw and slide the square into the slits at other end of the straw.

4 Push the straight pin through the middle of the straw and into the pencil eraser. Make sure there is space between the straw and eraser; you don't want them to touch.

5 Stand the pencil up in a large ball of play dough, or fill a container with sand or soil and stand the pencil up in it.

CONTINUED →

MAKE A WEATHER VANE *CONTINUED*

6 Put the ball of play dough or container in the center of the paper plate.

7 Label the plate like a compass rose with "North," "East," "South," and "West."

8 Take the weather vane outside and set it down so the north side of the plate faces the north. Use a compass to find north or use the sun (page 4) to find the right direction. Watch as the wind blows the arrow. It will point to the direction the wind is coming from. This is because the larger square catches the wind.

9 Which direction is the wind blowing? What does that suggest about the temperature and humidity that is blowing your way? Remember, if the direction changes suddenly, it means rain or a storm is heading your way.

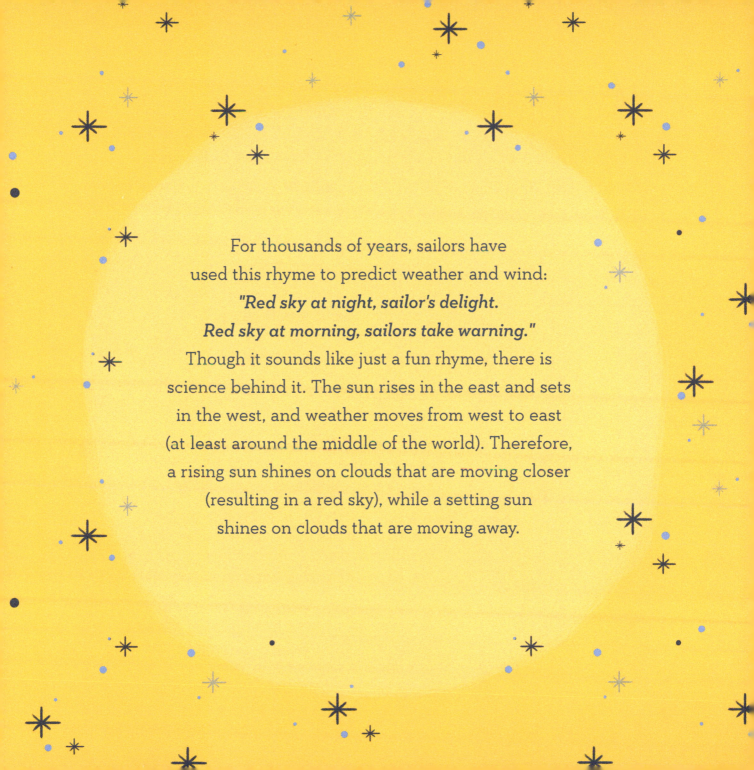

For thousands of years, sailors have
used this rhyme to predict weather and wind:
"Red sky at night, sailor's delight.
Red sky at morning, sailors take warning."
Though it sounds like just a fun rhyme, there is
science behind it. The sun rises in the east and sets
in the west, and weather moves from west to east
(at least around the middle of the world). Therefore,
a rising sun shines on clouds that are moving closer
(resulting in a red sky), while a setting sun
shines on clouds that are moving away.

MAKE A KITE

Flying a kite on a windy day is a great way for Adventure Girls to run around outside and enjoy nature. Making your own gives you a chance for some hands-on, creative fun.

WHAT YOU'LL NEED

6 plastic straws

Scissors

Tape

Ball of string or yarn

Large plastic bag

1 Start with six plastic straws. Cut one in half.

2 Connect three straws together by pinching the end of one straw and putting it inside the end of another straw. Use tape to secure where the straws are connected.

3 Now connect two and a half straws together. Use tape to secure where the straws are connected.

4 Arrange the straws in a cross shape, with the longer piece going up and down and the shorter piece going across it. Tape the pieces together where they touch in the middle.

5 Now you will create the outside of the kite frame with string or yarn. Cut slits in the four outer straw ends.

6 Starting at the bottom, slide the string in between the slits. Continue around to each corner, tucking the string into the slits, until you get back to the bottom. Tie the string together in a knot to finish, and cut off any extra.

7 Cut apart a large plastic bag so you have one large plastic sheet. You could use a large shopping bag or a garbage bag.

8 Put the kite frame on top of the plastic bag. Trim the plastic bag so it is 1 inch larger than the kite frame all the way around.

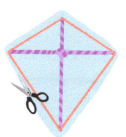

9 Fold the extra inch of bag over the string frame and tape it down. Continue folding and taping the bag around the frame.

10 Cut a piece of string that is double the width of the kite. Tie one end to the right side of the frame and tie the other end to the left side of the frame.

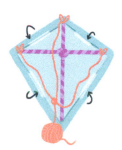

11 Take a very long piece of string and tie one end to the top of the frame. Loop it once around the other string in the middle and you are ready to fly your kite.

MAKE A WIND CHIME

Wind chimes can make so many beautiful sounds depending on which materials you use. You can hang yours on your porch, outside a window, or even inside where you can enjoy looking at your beautiful creation every day.

WHAT YOU'LL NEED

Large plastic lid

Hammer and a nail (ask a parent for permission first)

Ruler (optional)

String or yarn

Scissors

Objects to make sound

Beads or buttons

1 Decide how many strings you want to hang from your wind chime. Take the plastic lid and make the same number of holes evenly around the outside edge by hammering a nail into the lid and then removing it.

2 Cut a 2-foot piece of string for each hole. If you don't have a ruler, measure the string from your wrist to your shoulder.

3 Use the hammer and nail to punch two more holes in the middle of the plastic lid.

4 To make the beautiful noise on your wind chime, you can use bottle caps, aluminum canning lids, pieces of wood—anything you can make a hole in with a hammer and nail. You can also use things you can tie to the string, like shells, spoons, or pencils.

5 If you are using pencils, shells, or spoons, tie the string around each item.

6 Use the hammer and nail to punch a hole in the remaining items. Thread the string through each hole and tie a knot.

7 Thread beads or buttons onto the strings above the items.

8 Thread the other end of each string through one of the holes on the plastic lid and tie it in a knot to secure it. Continue until all of the strings are full and attached to the plastic lid.

9 Thread a long piece of string through each of the two middle holes in the plastic lid. Gather the two ends at the top and tie them in a knot so your wind chime can hang from it.

ANIMAL TRACKS

Whether you are in your yard, at the park, or on a hike, you can find signs of different animals that have been nearby.

LOOK FOR FOOTPRINTS

Use the chart to help you identify what animal prints you've seen.

BEAR

CAT

DEER

DOG

WOLF

MOUSE

OPOSSUM

RABBIT

IS IT A DOG OR A WOLF?

Dog prints and wolf prints can be so similar that they are hard to tell apart, but there are a few small differences between dog prints and wolf prints that can help you figure out which one has been nearby.

SIZE: Wolves have larger tracks, usually 4 or 5 inches. Dog tracks are smaller.

PATH: Wolves move in very straight lines; dogs tend to move right and left as they move down their path.

DOG TRACKS   **WOLF TRACKS**

LOOKING FOR OTHER SIGNS

Animal tracks aren't the only way to know if an animal has been nearby. If you look closely you will see other signs. You may see feathers or nests from birds or nibbled nuts or leaves from squirrels. Scratch marks on trees are a sign that animals with antlers or claws were there. Animal droppings can give you a clue to whether the animal is big or small. You may even see pieces of fur, skin, or bones left behind by animals. Take pictures or note your findings in a journal so that you can identify different animals.

NATURE PRINTS IN DOUGH

Experiment by making your own prints using salt dough. Try making prints with your finger, your dog's paw, a shell, a leaf, a flower, or even a coin!

WHAT YOU'LL NEED

Bowl

1 cup salt

1 cup flour

½ cup water

Parchment paper or wax paper

1   In a large bowl, mix salt, flour, and water until dough forms.

2   Take a handful of dough and use your hands to flatten it into a circle. Put the circle of dough on parchment or wax paper so it doesn't stick.

3   Make a print in the dough by taking your item and firmly pressing it into the dough, then lifting it out. For example, to make a leaf print, lay your leaf on the dough and press. Then carefully lift the leaf from the dough to see the print it leaves behind.

4   If you aren't happy with the way your print turned out, roll the dough into a ball and then flatten it to try again.

5   Once you are happy with your print, leave it out for several days to let the dough harden. You can speed up the drying process by baking it (ask a parent's permission) at 200°F for 2 hours.

MAKE A NATURE JOURNAL

Make your own nature journal to take with you on your outdoor adventures. You can use it to take notes about what you see and learn, or to write about the fun you have on your hikes.

WHAT YOU'LL NEED

1 piece of 8½ x 11-inch card stock or thick construction paper

Scissors

White or lined paper

Hole punch

Stick

Rubber band

1   Fold a piece of card stock or thick construction paper in half. This will be the front and back cover.

2   Cut pieces of plain white or lined paper for the inside of the journal. This paper should be the same size as the front and back cover.

3   Take the cover and punch 2 holes on the left edge, one hole about an inch from the top and another hole about an inch from the bottom.

4   Using the cover as your guide, punch matching holes in the rest of the paper.

5   Find a straight stick that is longer than the distance between the two holes. This will keep the nature journal together.

6 Wrap the rubber band around the top of the stick. Thread the other end of the rubber band through the top holes of the cover and paper.

7 Pull the end of the rubber band along the backside of the journal and up through the bottom holes of the paper.

8 Wrap that end of the rubber band around the bottom of the stick.

9 On the front of your journal you will see the stick with a loop around the top and the bottom of it. On the back of your journal you will see a rubber band stretched between the two holes.

10 Now your journal is secure and ready for writing.

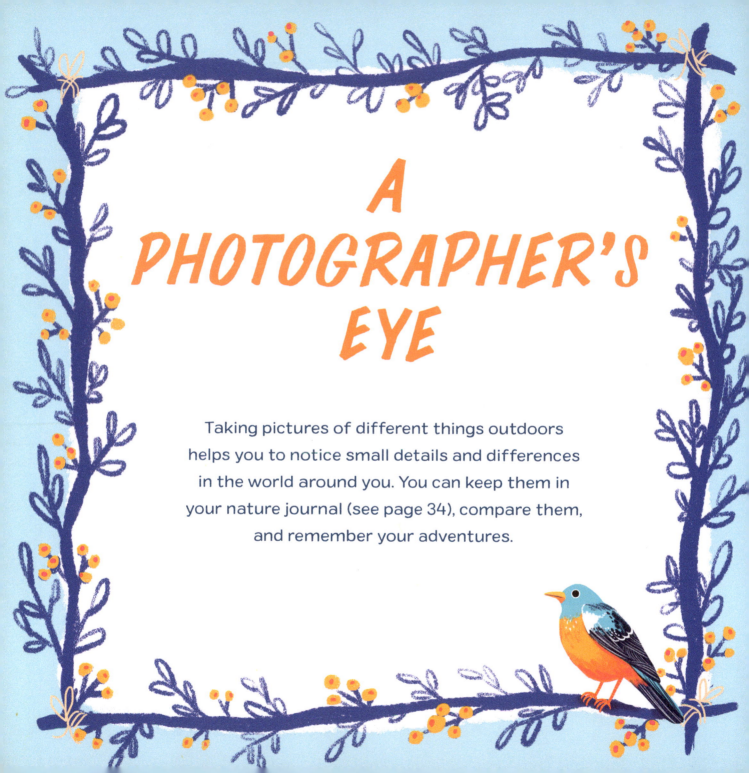

A PHOTOGRAPHER'S EYE

Taking pictures of different things outdoors
helps you to notice small details and differences
in the world around you. You can keep them in
your nature journal (see page 34), compare them,
and remember your adventures.

TIPS FOR TAKING NATURE PHOTOS

Taking great nature photographs takes practice, but here are some tips to give you a strong start.

DETERMINE YOUR SUBJECT. Decide what you want to take a picture of: maybe a flower or plant, an animal, clouds, or even the sunset. You can take pictures from your porch or yard, a spot in your neighborhood, at the park, or while you're on a walk.

FRAME THE PHOTO. Pay attention to what else can be seen in the picture with your subject. Is it a distraction? If it is, move to a different spot. Try taking the picture from farther away or closer up. Try taking it from either side to get the best shot. What you are taking a picture of doesn't always need to be in the middle of the frame; it can be off to one side.

TRY DIFFERENT VIEWPOINTS. You can take pictures from different angles. Try getting down low on the ground to take your picture, climb up a little and take a picture from above, get a close-up of something small, or get face-to-face with your family pet.

PHOTOGRAPH ANIMALS. To take a picture of an animal, whether it is your family pet, a bird, or a wild animal, make sure to be still and quiet. Be patient and wait for the right moment. You can be farther away and zoom in to get a close shot without disturbing the animal. You can try to capture a cool action shot or a picture of the animal being still.

CONSIDER LIGHTING. The best light to take photographs is in the early morning or in the evening, before the sunset. Cloudy days are also great. If it is sunny, try to take the picture with the sun behind your back.

MAKE A PINHOLE CAMERA

The pinhole camera was invented thousands of years ago and helped prove that light travels in a straight line. It is the simplest camera that can be made. Make your own pinhole camera and experiment with light and how the camera works.

WHAT YOU'LL NEED

Wax paper

2 toilet paper tubes

Tape

Aluminum foil

Thumbtack, pin, or nail

1 Fit a piece of wax paper over the end of one toilet paper tube. Pull it tight and tape it to the tube to secure it.

2 Fit a piece of aluminum foil over the end of the other toilet paper tube. Pull it tight and tape it to the tube to secure it.

3 Use a thumbtack or pin to poke a tiny hole in the center of the aluminum foil.

4 Put the aluminum foil end of the tube on the table. Put the wax paper end of the tube on top of the aluminum foil tube. Tape them together.

5 Roll the pinhole camera (except the ends) in aluminum foil and tape to secure it.

6 Now experiment with the pinhole camera. Point it toward a light or take it outside and look around. Look into the open end and point the pinhole toward what you want to see.

7 The images will appear upside down. In a camera, the film would be where your eye is and the image would be recorded on it.

STEPS 1 & 2

STEP 3

STEP 4

ADVENTURE GIRL CHALLENGE

Photography tells a story. It can tell a story about how you are feeling, an event that has happened, or a memory of something special. Take five pictures that tell a story.

TYING KNOTS

Knowing how to tie knots comes in handy while you are on adventures. You can use knots to attach gear to a backpack, carry a bundle of sticks, or tie two ropes together to make a longer one.

SQUARE KNOT

The square knot can be used to hold two objects together.

WHAT YOU'LL NEED

2 pieces of rope

1 Take two pieces of rope. We'll call them Rope 1 and Rope 2.

2 Cross Rope 1 over Rope 2.

3 Wrap Rope 1 under Rope 2.

4 Bring Rope 1 back over Rope 2. (So far, this is just like starting to tie your shoes.)

5 Cross Rope 1 over Rope 2.

6 Pull Rope 1 under Rope 2.

7 Pull both ends to tighten.

STEPS 1, 2, 3

STEPS 4, 5, 6

STEP 7

SHEET BEND

Use the sheet bend knot to tie two ropes together, even if they are different sizes or widths.

WHAT YOU'LL NEED

2 pieces of rope

1 Take two pieces of rope. We'll call them Rope 1 and Rope 2.

2 Make an open loop with Rope 1.

3 Pass Rope 2 through the loop of Rope 1 from underneath.

4 Wrap Rope 2 around Rope 1 from underneath and tuck it under itself.

5 Pull both sides to tighten.

STEPS 1 & 2

STEPS 3 & 4

STEP 5

KNOT BRACELETS

Use what you've learned about tying square knots to make a really cool bracelet. Experiment with using different colors to make a special bracelet for yourself or for a friend.

WHAT YOU'LL NEED

String, braiding cord, twine, yarn, or embroidery floss

Scissors

Tape

1 Cut two pieces of string, each about 4 feet long.

2 Gather the two pieces together evenly and fold them in half. This will make a loop at the top.

3 Hold the loop, wrap it around your finger, tuck the loop under the string, and pull to make a knot. You now have four strings hanging from the knot.

4 Tape the knot to a hard surface, like a table.

KNOT BRACELETS *CONTINUED*

5 Spread the four strings apart and pick up the two middle pieces. Keeping them together in the center, pull tight and tape them to the table (closer to the end of the string). You now have two loose strings, one on the left and one on the right.

6 Pick up the string on the left and cross it over the two center strings, in an L shape.

7 Pick up the string on the right and cross it under the two center strings, making sure it is going over the top of the left string. Bring it through the left loop.

8 Pull both strings evenly to tighten the knot.

9 Pick up the right string and cross it over the two center strings, in a backwards L shape.

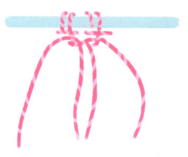

10 Take the string on the left and cross it under the two center strings, making sure it is going over the top of the right string. Bring it through the right loop.

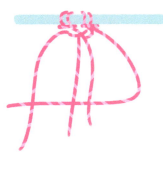

11 Pull both strings evenly to tighten the knot.

12 Repeat steps 6 to 11 to keep making square knots. Continue until you form the length you want (long enough to be tied on a wrist as a bracelet or used as a keychain).

13 To finish, gather all four strings, wrap them around your finger, tuck them through the loop, and pull to create a finishing knot.

ADVENTURE GIRL CHALLENGE

Make a dog or cat toy! You'll need four 2-inch wide pieces of fleece that are about 4 feet long. Tie the strips in a knot near the top and follow the same steps as the square knot bracelet.

A BACKYARD HIDEAWAY

A backyard hideaway is a special place
that you can design, build, and spend time in.
It is a place that you can make your own and
make changes to whenever you want.

BUILD A SHELTER

Building a shelter is a fun challenge. It can be done quickly with a few materials or you can spend days making it exactly how you want it.

WHAT YOU'LL NEED

Large sticks or branches

Trees

Grass

1 Look for a place for your shelter. You need an area that is cleared out so it is easy for you to get to. You also need a good base for the shelter, like two branches that form a Y shape, two trees that are close together, or a fence.

2 Gather large sticks or branches that have already fallen from trees. (You never want to harm a tree or bush by cutting or ripping off its branches.)

3 Start by leaning the ends of the largest sticks or branches in the Y of the tree or against the fence. Think about making a tent or triangle shape.

4 Continue to add more sticks to form the walls of your shelter.

CONTINUED →

BUILD A SHELTER *CONTINUED*

5 When you are happy with the size and shape of your shelter, cover the openings with tall grass or leafy branches.

6 If you like, you can cover the ground inside your shelter with grass, leaves, hay, or cardboard.

> **⋛ FUN TIP ⋜**
> Turn your shelter into a secret clubhouse. What will your club be called? What are the rules? Who will be in it?

HIDEOUT

BUILD AN AIR FORT

Create an indoor shelter by building your very own air fort. Sit in it to read and write in, play a game, or just relax.

WHAT YOU'LL NEED

Box fan

Heavy-duty tape

Bedsheet

1 Ask a parent's permission to use a box fan.

2 Use heavy-duty tape like duct tape or packaging tape to attach a sheet to the top and sides of the box fan.

3 Tape the opposite corners of the sheet to the floor.

4 Turn the fan on to create a huge room under the sheet.

ADVENTURE GIRL CHALLENGE

Use chairs, cushions, and blankets to create an indoor fort. How big can you make it? How many rooms can it have?

STARGAZING

The night sky is fascinating! From constellations to planets, there is always something new to learn and see.

LOOKING FOR PLANETS

You can actually tell the difference between a planet and a star without a telescope. Stars twinkle and shimmer. Planets do not. Planets are closer to Earth, so they seem to be in an oval shape instead of tiny dots.

There are five planets you can see from Earth without a telescope because they are brighter than the stars around them: Mercury, Venus, Mars, Jupiter, and Saturn. Jupiter and Saturn are the easiest to see.

You will see planets best when you are in country areas, away from city lights that can limit your view of the night sky. It is helpful to look just as it is starting to get dark outside at night, or as it is starting to get light again early in the morning. You can go online to EarthSky.org for more tips on when and where to get the best view of planets.

Now you can host a stargazing party! Lay out blankets or set up chairs and invite your friends and family over to watch the stars with you. Point out constellations or even make up some of your own.

TIPS FOR IDENTIFYING PLANETS

- **MERCURY** is a gray or brownish color.
- **VENUS** is a light yellow color.
- **MARS** looks pink or red depending on where it is and its brightness.
- **JUPITER** looks orange with lines.
- **SATURN** is gold.

CONSTELLATIONS

Constellations are groups of stars that create patterns in the sky. Each star is a part of one constellation. Sometimes it seems like constellations have moved to a different spot in the sky. This is because the earth travels around the sun. It takes constellations a full year to change positions across the night sky from east to west.

Thousands of years ago, constellations helped people keep track of the seasons. They helped hunters gauge when animals were hibernating and helped farmers know when to plant their crops.

Constellations are also used to identify and name stars and to find which direction you are traveling. The best way to learn more is to go outside at the same time every night and observe the sky. You can use books, websites, or apps to help you identify constellations.

URSA MAJOR (THE BIG DIPPER)

Ursa Major is the third largest constellation. People often call it the Big Dipper, but the Big Dipper is only a small piece of Ursa Major. The Big Dipper looks like a big bowl with a spoon in it and is well known because it includes the seven brightest stars of Ursa Major. In spring and summer, the Big Dipper is high overhead. In fall and winter, it appears lower and closer to the horizon.

URSA MINOR (THE LITTLE DIPPER)

Ursa Minor is a large constellation. Seven of its brightest stars are the easiest to see. They form the Little Dipper, which looks like a bowl with a spoon in it. The last star of the Little Dipper is the brightest one and is named Polaris, or the North Star. It always points north and can help you find your way.

ORION

Orion (see page 5) is one of the largest constellations in the sky. It is most visible from November to February and is one of the easier constellations to locate because of three very bright stars in a row called Orion's Belt.

TAURUS

Taurus is sometimes called "The Bull." It is best seen during December and January. Its brightest star is a "red giant" called Aldebaran. Aldebaran is the fourteenth brightest star in the sky.

GEMINI

Gemini is easiest to see during January and February. It looks like two stick people holding hands. There are 85 stars in this constellation that you can see without a telescope.

3-D STARS

Let the night sky inspire you. Decorate your room with three-dimensional stars. You can hang them from your ceiling or set them on a shelf. You can even arrange them like a constellation.

WHAT YOU'LL NEED

Decorative paper

Scratch paper (for template)

Pencil

Scissors

Glue or tape

Hole punch

String (optional)

1 Use a piece of colored paper or decorate a piece of paper with a design that you'd like on your stars.

2 Draw a star outline on a piece of scratch paper or print one from your computer.

3 Cut out the star.

4 Trace that star template on the decorative paper four times and cut out those stars.

5 Fold all four of the decorative stars in half.

STEPS 2 & 3

STEPS 4 & 5

STEP 6

6 Glue the back of the right side of a star to the back of a left side of a different star. Repeat this step, until all of the stars are added in and glued in a circle.

7 Punch a hole in the top, thread a string through the hole and tie it in a knot. Your three-dimensional star is ready to hang.

> ⇝ *FUN TIP* ⇜
> Try cutting your stars from aluminum foil instead of paper.

DOWN IN THE DIRT

There are bugs living all over the world in forests, in water, underground, and on mountaintops. They are different sizes, colors, and shapes. But not all bugs are considered insects.

CLASSIFYING INSECTS

Did you know that there are one million different types of insects on the earth? That doesn't even include spiders, because spiders aren't actually considered insects. There are four things that make a bug an insect.

SIX LEGS: All insects have only six legs. If it has fewer legs or more, it is not considered an insect.

EXOSKELETON: All insects have an exoskeleton, which is a hard shell that covers its body.

THREE BODY PARTS: All insects have three body parts: a head, thorax, and abdomen.

ANTENNAE: Insects have one pair of antennae.

Get outside and observe the bugs around you, Adventure Girls! Are the bugs you come across considered insects? Write down what you find.

THE WORLD'S WEIRDEST INSECTS

Take time to research some of the world's weirdest insects. The giant weta is the largest insect in the world, and the Hercules beetle can carry 800 times its weight. You might find the walking stick interesting because it can grow back any legs that it loses. The praying mantis eats bees, butterflies, mice, and small birds. What weird insects can you discover?

MAKE YOUR OWN MAGNIFYING GLASS

Magnifying glasses are used to enlarge the details of tiny objects up close. Make your own and use it to observe tiny creatures in your area.

WHAT YOU'LL NEED

Clear plastic bottle

Marker

Scissors

Water

1. Find a clear plastic bottle, such as a two-liter soda bottle. It is important for the plastic to be clear and smooth.

2. Starting right under the opening of the bottle, draw a circle (about the size of the top of a cup).

3. Ask an adult to help you cut out the circle. The piece of plastic you cut out will have a slight curve in it because of the part of the bottle you cut it from.

STEPS 1 & 2

STEP 3

STEP 4

4 Put several drops of water onto the plastic piece.

5 Your magnifying glass is ready. Test it out by holding it over a book. Notice how the print looks bigger through the water. This works because the water bends the light traveling through the plastic.

6 Now use your magnifying glass to observe tiny insects or bugs.

STEPS 5 & 6

ADVENTURE GIRL CHALLENGE

Invent and draw your own insect. Where does it live? What color is it? What does it eat and what eats it? Try making a 3-D model of it with dough like you used when making Nature Prints (see page 33).

MAKE A BUG HOTEL

You can learn so much by observing insects. Make a bug hotel to take a closer look and to give them a safe place to stay.

WHAT YOU'LL NEED

Empty can or plastic drink container

Scissors (optional)

Natural materials from outside

1 Find an empty container, like a can, that you can use to make a bug hotel. If you are using a plastic container, cut the top off so you have a larger opening and a cylinder shape.

2 Turn the container on its side so it is lying on the ground.

3 Gather natural items such as sticks, rocks, pinecones, grass, or tree bark.

4 Layer the natural items inside the cylinder. Pack them in as tight as you can so they will stay in the container, but insects will still have room to crawl in and spaces to hide.

5 Keep your bug hotel on its side and find a special place for it. It can be on the ground or hanging (wrap string around your container to hang it).

6 Frequently check back to see if you have any bugs living in the hotel and observe them.

**MARGARET JAMES
STRICKLAND COLLINS** (1922–1996)
knew everything there was to know about
termites. Her astonishing knowledge earned her an
unusual nickname . . . The Termite Lady. As a little girl,
Margaret would find insects in the woods and bring them
home to study. Her father challenged her to use books
to identify them, which ignited her desire to learn as
much as she could about bugs. She kept up these studies
throughout her life and eventually became the first
female African American entomologist (a scientist
who studies insects) and the third Black female
zoologist in the United States.

BIRD WATCHING

Some people think that the way a bird looks is the only thing that makes it unique, but each type of bird is actually very different from the others, from the sounds they make and the nests they build, to the special qualities that make them able to live in a specific area.

MAKE A BIRDHOUSE

Give your feathered friends a special place near your home where you can observe and learn about them. You can sketch, write about, or take photos of the birds you see.

WHAT YOU'LL NEED

Gallon milk jug or large juice container

Scissors

String or rope

Natural materials from outside

Glue

1 Use scissors to carefully make a hole on each side of the container toward the top, near the lid. You might need to ask an adult for help.

2 Thread your string or rope through the holes and tie it in a secure knot at the top.

3 Cut a 3-inch circle in the middle of the container's front. The birds will use this hole to enter the house. You might need to ask an adult to help get you started. Gather materials from outside, such as leaves, sticks, pieces of bark, and grass. Glue the items around the outside of the birdhouse to make it more inviting for a bird to build its nest.

4 Hang the birdhouse from a tree and wait. Don't get frustrated if a bird doesn't start using it right away. Sometimes it can take a few months.

FEATHERED FLYERS

It's always a treat to see a rare bird, but knowing what common birds look like is important, too. Here are six birds that you are likely to see around your home or town that you can learn to identify.

ROBINS are often the first birds you see in the spring, no matter where you live. Robins build round nests in trees and their eggs are light blue. They like to eat earthworms from the ground.

CROWS have shiny black feathers. They prefer open areas with a lot of trees and live on almost every continent. They are smart birds. They use their "caw" to communicate with each other. They eat meat and plants.

BLUE JAYS live in forests, but you might also see them at your backyard bird feeder. They often bury food to eat later. Blue jays are slow flyers, but are protective of their nests and food and often chase other birds away.

STARLINGS nest in trees. They have strong feet and walk on the ground a lot. These noisy birds help farmers by eating insects that sometimes hurt their crops, but they can also be a problem for farmers when they eat their fruit.

NUTHATCHES nest in cavities inside trees. They have strong legs and can walk up and down on a tree trunk. Nuthatches are smart and use a piece of bark from a tree as a tool to hunt for insects.

CROW

BLUE JAY

ROBIN

NUTHATCH

STARLING

BUILD A BIRD FEEDER

Bird feeders come in all shapes and sizes. If it can hold birdseed or mealworms, then it is the perfect feeder for a bird. Try making one from wooden craft sticks.

WHAT YOU'LL NEED

50 craft sticks

Glue

String

Birdseed or mealworms

1   Lay eight craft sticks side by side, all touching.

2   Glue two craft sticks in the opposite direction, one on each side. This is the base of the birdfeeder.

3   Flip over the base so the two craft sticks you just glued are on the bottom.

4   Lay eight more craft sticks on top of the base in the opposite direction of the first eight. Glue those eight craft sticks down. This will keep the birdseed from falling out.

5   Now you will use the rest of the craft sticks to build a wall around the outer edge of the base that will hold the birdseed in. Glue one stick on the top edge of the square and one stick on the bottom edge of the square.

6 Glue one stick on the left edge of the square and one stick on the right edge of the square.

7 Keep gluing sticks on all four sides until the wall is about eight sticks tall.

8 Let the glue dry.

9 Thread a piece of string through the sticks on the right side. Make a loop and tie it in a knot at the top.

10 Thread a piece of string through the sticks on the left side. Make a loop and tie it in a knot at the top.

11 Hang the bird feeder from the string on a tree.

12 Fill it with birdseed or mealworms and enjoy watching the birds come to eat.

RECYCLED BIRD FEEDER

Reuse a plastic lid by turning it into a bird feeder in just a few quick steps.

WHAT YOU'LL NEED

Hole puncher

Plastic lid

String

Peanut butter

Birdseed or crushed cereal

1 Punch a hole in the top of a plastic lid.

2 Thread the string through the hole and secure it with a knot.

3 Fill the lid with peanut butter.

4 Press birdseed into the peanut butter. If you don't have birdseed, you can use crushed cereal.

5 Hang the bird feeder and watch the birds fly over for a treat.

FUN TIP

If you don't have a plastic lid, you can use an empty toilet paper tube. Use a butter knife to cover it with peanut butter and press the birdseed or crushed cereal onto it.

ADVENTURE GIRL CHALLENGE

Gather natural materials from outside. Wrap and weave your materials together to form a nest the way a bird would. You can use your nest as a decoration or put it in a nearby tree to see if it attracts a bird.

Since she was a little girl,
FRANCES HAMERSTROM (1907–1998)
was devoted to learning about and protecting
animals. Her father didn't always approve of her
adventures, so she planted poison ivy to hide where she
kept her wilderness gear. It was no surprise when Frances
grew up to become an ornithologist—a scientist who studies
birds. She and her husband spent more than 40 years
observing the greater prairie chicken, which was on its
way to extinction. They are credited with preventing
this fascinating species from dying out
in the state of Wisconsin.

MAKE IT FLOAT

Why do some things float and others sink? Figuring out a way to make things float is a fun challenge that Adventure Girls can conquer!

FLOATING EGG EXPERIMENT

Are you ready for some fun with science? Discover what happens when you change the density of water by adding salt.

WHAT YOU'LL NEED

2 clear cups

Water

2 eggs

8 spoonfuls salt

Spoon

1 Fill two clear cups with water.

2 Put an egg in the first cup of water. What happens to the egg?

3 Put the salt into the second glass of water. Stir.

4 Put the second egg in the salt water. What happens to this egg?

5 Does the same thing happen with different objects? Try this experiment with a penny, a small rock, or an eraser.

ADVENTURE GIRL CHALLENGE

Try building a boat with aluminum foil, sticks, paper, sponges, or corks. Does it float? Can it hold weight?

BUILD A STICK RAFT

Create a floating raft from sticks and see how much weight it can hold and how fast it can travel. Make two rafts and have a race on a windy day.

WHAT YOU'LL NEED

9 sticks, all 6 inches long and about the same thickness (slightly thicker than a pencil)

2 pieces of string, yarn, or twine, about 3 feet long

Scissors

Construction paper or fabric

Hot glue gun

1 Pick one stick and securely tie a string to each end. The knots should be about a half-inch from each end of the stick.

2 Put another stick next to the first one. Take the string on each end and wrap it around the second stick three times. Keep the sticks as close together as possible, but don't worry there is a small gap between them. Keep the string as tight as you can.

3 Continue adding sticks, wrapping each with the string three times on both ends.

4 After adding the eighth stick, tie all eight sticks tightly together. Cut off any extra string from the ends.

5 To add a sail, cut a piece of paper or fabric in the shape of a square or a triangle. Use a glue gun to secure the sail to the last stick. Wedge the stick upright between two sticks of the raft. You can use a hot glue gun to secure it.

6 Test out your stick raft. Does it float? Can it hold weight?

NEIGHBORHOOD GAMES

Playing games with friends and family is a fun way to spend your day! Teach these games to your friends and let the adventures begin!

CAPTURE THE FLAG

Teamwork, strategy, and a little sneakiness will help you in this exciting game.

WHAT YOU'LL NEED

Friends

Chalk or cones (optional)

Flags, bandanas, fabric, or old shirts

1 Split the players into two teams.

2 Decide on the boundaries of the game area. The bigger the area you have to play, the better. You might want to mark the boundaries with chalk or cones, or just make invisible boundaries between trees.

3 Divide the area in half. Find a way to mark the halfway line. Each half is "home base" for one team.

4 Each team hides their flag somewhere in their area. Part of the flag has to be showing.

5 When the game begins, the players race to capture the other team's flag.

6 If a player is on their own side of the halfway line, they are safe and cannot be tagged. If they go onto the other team's half, they can be tagged out.

CONTINUED →

CAPTURE THE FLAG *CONTINUED*

7 If you are tagged on the other team's side, go out of bounds and wait. Once a player from the other team is tagged and sits out, you get to go back in.

8 There is no flag guarding. All players must be 10 feet away from their flag.

9 The first team to capture the flag and bring it back to their side wins.

FREEZE DANCE

Even if you're trapped inside on a rainy day, you can play games to stay active . . . and warm!

WHAT YOU'LL NEED

Friends

Music

1 Choose a friend to be in charge of turning the music on and off for the first round.

2 When the music goes on, everyone starts dancing—the crazier the better.

3 When the music turns off, everyone freezes. Anyone caught still moving is out.

4 The last one on the floor becomes the new music master!

THREE FLIES UP

You can play this game almost anywhere as long as you have a group of people and a ball.

WHAT YOU'LL NEED

Friends

Soft kickball, baseball, football, or beanbag

1. Decide who will be the thrower and where the thrower will stand. The rest of the players will gather a good distance away (about 20 yards).

2. The thrower stands in the designated area and throws the ball underhand, high into the air. The players try to catch the ball.

3. When you catch a ball you score one point. Each player keeps track of her own points.

4. When a player catches three balls, they win and it is their turn to be the thrower.

5. For more of a challenge, the thrower can have her back turned to the players waiting to catch the ball.

SARDINES

Sardines is similar to the classic game Hide and Seek, but with a twist.

WHAT YOU'LL NEED

4 or more friends

1 One person is the "hider." Everyone else closes their eyes and counts to 30 while she hides.

2 When a player finds the hider, instead of telling everyone where she is hiding, she quietly hides with her.

3 As each new player finds the group, they hide with them.

4 The last player to find the hiding spot becomes the new hider.

ADVENTURE GIRL CHALLENGE

Make an obstacle course in your yard or at the park and challenge a friend to race you.

WILMA RUDOLPH (1940–1994)
was the first woman to win three gold
medals in Track and Field events during
one Olympics. When Wilma was younger
she had trouble with her left leg and
had to wear a brace on it. She overcame
those challenges and is remembered as
one of the fastest women in track and an
inspiration to all athletes.

SHADOW THEATER

More than 2,000 years ago, shadow theaters were invented in Asia. They used oil lamps to light the theater before electricity was invented, and they included different voices and music in their performances. They helped tell stories that all people could enjoy or learn from, even if they spoke different languages.

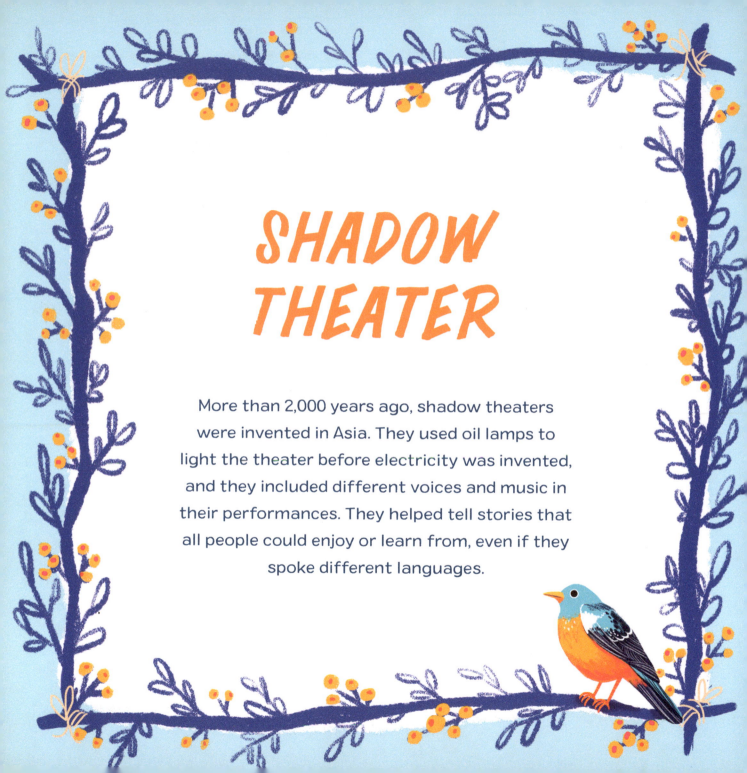

BUILD YOUR THEATER

Get creative with light and shadows by making a shadow theater.

WHAT YOU'LL NEED

Cardboard box, like a shoebox, shipping box, or cereal box

Marker

Scissors

Thin white paper or wax paper

Tape

Light source, such as a flashlight, headlamp, or desk lamp

1 One side of your box should already be open. That will be the back of your theater.

2 Use the marker to draw a rectangle on the opposite side of the box. Leave a 1-inch border on all of the sides. Imagine this side looking like a TV screen.

3 Cut out the rectangle.

4 Replace the rectangle that you just cut out with a thin white piece of paper or wax paper. Tape the paper to the box.

5 Now your theater is ready.

CONTINUED →

STEP 1

STEPS 2 & 3

STEP 4

BUILD YOUR THEATER *CONTINUED*

6 Shine the light source from the back of the theatre toward the front. Turn all other lights off.

7 Use your hands or shadow puppets to tell a story by putting them between the light and the box. The closer they are to the white paper in the front, the better.

CREATE SHADOW PUPPETS

Design your own shadow puppets and let the storytelling begin.

WHAT YOU'LL NEED

Marker

Cardboard or black construction paper

Scissors

Tape

Straws or craft sticks

1 Draw or trace the outline of animals, people, or other shapes onto cardboard or black construction paper.

2 Cut out the shapes.

3 Tape a straw or craft stick to the back of your shape.

4 Experiment with your puppets by putting them between the light and the front of the shadow theater.

5 Retell a story you already know, or make up your own.

ADVENTURE GIRL CHALLENGE

Write your own script and use your shadow theater and puppets to perform it. Try to include three characters, a problem, and how the problem gets solved. Does your story have a happy ending? Perform your story for family or friends.

⇒ FUN TIP ⇐
You can also use stickers as shadow puppets by sticking them onto craft sticks or straws.

SPICE IT UP

Growing and cooking with herbs is another fun—and tasty!—way for Adventure Girls to interact with nature. And planting and tending seeds is a great chance to see science in action. You can write about what you learn and observe in your nature journal (page 34).

HOW TO GROW AN HERB GARDEN

Some of the easiest herbs to grow are basil, oregano, rosemary, thyme, parsley, and mint. Starting an herb garden from seeds can be done, but it is easier to start your garden with herb plants that have already sprouted.

WHAT YOU'LL NEED

Herb seedlings

Garden fork or shovel

Soil

Water

1   Figure out where to plant the herbs. They need a lot of sun. However, if you live in a place that is really hot (more than 80 degrees most days), plant your herbs in a place that only gets direct sun for 4 to 6 hours.

2   Prepare the soil by loosening it with a garden fork or shovel. This is an important step because it allows water to drain and roots to grow.

3   To take the seedling plant out of its starter container, turn it upside down and tap the bottom while you gently hold the base of the stems.

4   Dig a hole and set the roots of the plant in it. Fill the hole with soil up to the base of the stem.

CONTINUED →

HOW TO GROW AN HERB GARDEN *CONTINUED*

5 Plant the next herb plant 1 to 2 feet away. Water the plants immediately after you plant them.

6 To see if the herbs need water, put your finger down into the soil. If it feels dry, water it. If it still feels moist, wait another day.

7 As the herbs grow it is important to harvest them often. Don't be afraid to cut off and use the herbs. This helps the plants.

FLAVOR YOUR FOOD

Use your new herbs to flavor your food. Wash and chop the herbs into small pieces and sprinkle them on before or after cooking.

BASIL: Sprinkle in spaghetti sauce or layer between tomatoes and cheese for a tasty appetizer.

OREGANO: Sprinkle on top of pizza or fish before baking.

ROSEMARY: Chop into very small pieces and mix in with potatoes, or sprinkle onto chicken before cooking.

MINT: Add to ice water, a fruit smoothie, or a fruit salad.

INDOOR GARDEN

If you don't have room for an outdoor garden, you can plant herbs in containers inside. Put them near the window or on the porch so they get enough sun and take care of them the same way you would if they were in the ground.

ADVENTURE GIRL CHALLENGE

Volunteer to make dinner for your family and season the food with your herbs. Ask an adult before using the oven or sharp utensils.

PAPER AIRPLANES

With a few quick folds of a piece of paper, you can make planes that glide, dive, and loop through the air.

THE CLASSIC AIRPLANE

1 Fold an 8½ x 11 inch piece of paper in half longways and unfold it.

2 Fold each of the top corners in toward the middle. They will meet at the centerline and there will be a point at the top.

3 Fold the paper in half the same way you did in step 1. Crease all of your edges really well.

4 On one side, fold down the wing so the top edge meets the bottom.

5 Flip over the plane and do the same thing on the other side, creating another wing.

6 Your plane is ready to fly.

STEP 1

STEP 2

STEP 3

STEPS 4 & 5

THE LIGHTNING BOLT

1 Fold an 8½ x 11 inch piece of paper in half longways and unfold it.

2 Fold each of the top corners in toward the middle. They will meet at the centerline.

3 Take the outside edges of the triangles and fold them in toward the middle again. They will meet at the centerline and will make a point at the end.

4 Fold the paper in half the same way you did in step 1. Crease all of your edges really well.

5 On one side, fold down the wing so the top edge meets the bottom.

6 Flip over the plane and do the same thing on the other side, creating another wing.

7 Your plane is ready to fly.

ADVENTURE GIRL CHALLENGE

Which paper airplane flies the farthest? Can you make any adjustments to the designs that will make them fly faster, farther, or higher?

STEP 1

STEP 2

STEP 3

STEP 4

STEPS 5 & 6

FLY YOUR PLANE!

THE SPACE FLYER

1 Fold an 8½ x 11 inch piece of paper in half longways and unfold it.

2 Fold the top edge down about 2 inches.

3 Fold the 2-inch section in half.

4 Now fold that section in half again. You will have a really small, thick fold at the top of your paper.

5 Flip the paper over so your folded section is still at the top, but on the underside of the paper.

6 Fold each of the top corners into the middle. They will meet at the centerline.

7 Fold the plane in half on the original crease. The thick folds that you made will be on the outside of the plane.

8 To make the wings, fold each side down as far as you can, leaving about ½ inch underneath the wing to grip the plane with.

9 Fold the edge of each wing up about 1 inch.

10 Your plane is ready to fly.

STEPS 1 & 2

STEP 3

STEP 4

STEPS 5 & 6

STEP 7

STEPS 8 & 9

MAKE YOUR OWN BOARD GAME

Adventures Girls are smart, clever, and like to have fun. Use your skills to make a board game so that everyone can have fun together. Want to take it a step further? Host a game night where everyone brings a game they've made themselves!

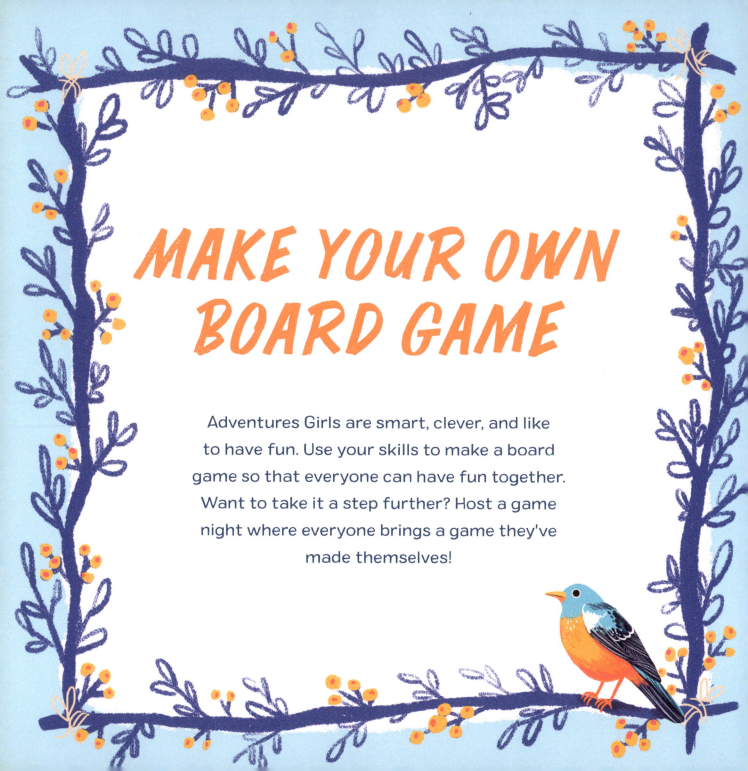

DESIGN YOUR GAME

WHAT YOU'LL NEED

Cardboard

Paper

Tape

Markers

Stickers (optional)

Glue (optional)

Scissors (optional)

Game Pieces (optional)

Binder clips (optional)

1 Decide the goal of your board game. Will it be to collect the most of something, to get to the finish line first, or to answer the most questions correctly?

2 Figure out if your game will use dice, cards, or both.

3 Create a theme for your game and design a game board to go with it. Use cardboard or tape pieces of paper together to make your game board.

4 Add details to your game with markers, stickers, or paper and glue, and make cards if needed.

5 Write a set of rules for your game board, including how to start and how a player wins.

6 Use game pieces from another game, turn small toys into game pieces, or make your own by drawing them and clipping them into a binder clip so they can stand up.

CLOWN AROUND

An Adventure Girl can brighten other people's day just being herself. You can also learn these cool tricks to make anyone smile.

LEARN TO JUGGLE

Learning this skill takes practice, but once you master it, you'll be able to juggle many different things.

1 START WITH ONE TISSUE IN YOUR RIGHT HAND. Toss the tissue from your right hand up toward your left hand. Catch it with your left hand. Toss it up with your left hand back toward your right hand and catch it. Get comfortable with this pattern before moving on.

2 NOW TRY TWO TISSUES, ONE IN EACH HAND. Toss the tissue from your right hand up toward your left hand. Before you can catch it with your left hand, toss that tissue up toward your right hand. Practice the rhythm: toss, toss, catch, catch. Next try three tissues, two in your right hand and one in your left. Toss one tissue from your right hand toward your left hand. Before you can catch it, throw that tissue up toward your right hand. Before you can catch it with your right hand, throw that tissue up toward your left hand. You should only have one tissue in each hand at a time. You are always tossing a tissue to empty your hand to catch the next one.

3 MASTER THIS RHYTHM WITH TISSUES SINCE THEY TRAVEL SLOWER. Once you are comfortable, trade the tissues for beanbags or balls.

ADVENTURE GIRL CHALLENGE

Host a night of magic and tricks for your friends and family. Practice your magic tricks, juggling, and balloon making as many times as possible before your performance and then wow your audience with your new skills.

MAKE A BALLOON DOG

Making a balloon animal isn't as tricky as it seems. Follow these steps to twist and turn your balloon into a dog.

WHAT YOU'LL NEED

Pencil balloon

Marker

1. Blow up a pencil balloon, leaving a few inches at the end uninflated. Tie off the balloon.

2. Make the dog's head by twisting three sections, each about 2 inches long, at the tied off end. When you are twisting the balloon, each section will stay if you twist it about three times.

3. Twist the first and third section together to make the dog's nose and ears.

4. After the head, twist three more sections. The first section will be shorter than the other two.

5. Now twist the last two sections together to make the front legs. There will be one section above the legs. That is the neck.

6 Twist three more sections (about 4 inches long). You now have four sections in a row.

7 Twist together the first and third sections to make the back legs and the tail.

8 Adjust the legs and head so they are all straight.

9 Draw a face and add details with your marker.

> ⟩ *FUN TIP* ⟨
>
> To make other balloon animals, all you need to do is make a few changes to the balloon dog. To make a giraffe, make the neck longer. Make a shorter neck and longer legs to form a horse.

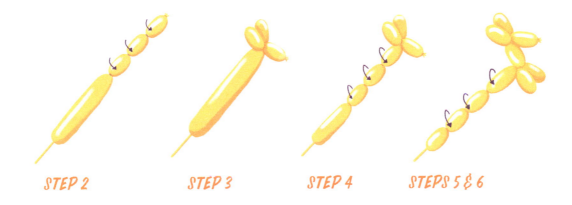

STEP 2   STEP 3   STEP 4   STEPS 5 & 6

MAGIC TRICKS

With any magic trick, there are two important steps: your preparation before the trick, and the story or movements you use during your trick.

PICK A CARD, ANY CARD

WHAT YOU'LL NEED

1 deck of cards

1   Before you are in front of an audience, prepare your deck by putting all of the red cards together and all of the black cards together. Put the two piles on top of one another.

2   Holding the deck of cards in your hands, fan several cards out from the top of your deck and ask your audience to "Pick a card, any card!"

3   Once they pull out a card (you will secretly know what color it is), ask them to remember the card.

4   Fan out the bottom part of the deck and have them place their card anywhere in the bottom.

5   Lightly shuffle your cards.

6   Turn the cards toward you and begin to fan them out. The card they picked will stand out to you because it will be a different color than all the cards around it.

DISAPPEARING TOOTHPICK

WHAT YOU'LL NEED

Clear tape

Toothpick

1 Use a small piece of clear tape to attach a toothpick to the top of your thumb. The top of the toothpick will be taped right below your fingernail. When you bend your thumb, the bottom half of the toothpick goes straight up into the air.

2 Tuck the bottom part of your thumb into your fist. The audience won't see that your thumb is tucked into your fingers, but will instead see you holding a toothpick in your fist.

3 Tell the audience that you need them to all say "hocus pocus" on the count of three.

4 Count to three and as they are saying the magic words, blow on your toothpick and quickly open both of your hands, the palms of your hands facing the audience. Be careful not to show the back of your thumb. Your audience will be amazed that their magic words and your quick breath made the toothpick disappear.

5 Practice this trick in the mirror several times before you do it in front of an audience. The best magicians have a clever story and make their hands move in ways that distract from the actual trick.

FUN WITH FLOWERS

Flowers, leaves, and herbs all have their own unique colors, scents, and qualities. Press flowers and herbs to keep as a special memory or to use in a craft or decoration.

PRESSING FLOWERS AND HERBS

WHAT YOU'LL NEED

Flowers, herbs, or leaves

Heavy books

Wax paper

Notebook paper

1 Pick flowers, leaves, or herbs to press.

2 Lay a book down and put a piece of wax paper on top of it.

3 Put a piece of notebook paper on top of the wax paper.

4 Place the flower or herb on top of the notebook paper.

5 Cover the flower or herb with another piece of notebook paper and a final piece of wax paper.

6 Lay several heavy books on top of the final piece of wax paper.

7 It will take about a week for the plant to completely dry out. Leave it pressed between the paper and books until then.

8 Every two days, lift off the top books and wax paper and replace the top piece of notebook paper. This will help absorb any moisture that is draining from the plant.

9 When the plant is flat and dried out, carefully remove it.

PRESSED FLOWER BOOKMARKS

Beautiful pressed flower bookmarks can be given as gifts or created as keepsakes with flowers from a special place.

WHAT YOU'LL NEED

Construction paper or card stock

Glue stick

Pressed flowers or herbs

Clear contact paper or a laminator

Scissors

Hole punch

Ribbon

1 Cut a bookmark-sized rectangle from card stock or construction paper.

2 Use a glue stick to add a small amount of glue; attach the pressed flowers or herbs to the bookmark.

3 Laminate the bookmark or cover it with clear contact paper. If you are using contact paper, lay the sticky side down on top of the pressed flowers and gently rub it down to seal it. Cut off any extra contact paper around the bookmark.

4 Punch a hole in the top of the bookmark.

5 Lace a piece of ribbon through the hole and tie it in a knot to secure it. Leave the ends hanging from the end of the bookmark as a decoration.

HAMMERED FLOWER AND LEAF PRINTS

Collect colorful flowers and leaves to make these prints. Experiment and create cool designs to use in different ways.

WHAT YOU'LL NEED

Old white T-shirt or light-colored fabric

Scissors

Flowers, leaves, or herbs

Hammer or rubber mallet (ask a parent for permission first)

1 Cut a piece of fabric from an old T-shirt.

2 Place a flower, leaf, or herb on the right side of the fabric.

3 Fold the fabric in half over the plant.

4 Hammer the fabric, aiming for where you placed the flower or leaf.

5 Hit the fabric several times with a hammer, tapping the entire area of the flower, and then open up the fabric. You will see colored prints from the plant.

6 Continue arranging different items on the fabric one at a time and hammering them to make a designed print.

7 Use the printed fabric to make a flag, wrap a present, or even as a hanging decoration.

ADVENTURE GIRL CHALLENGE

Use pressed flowers and herbs to create a design to frame and hang up, or make a pretty card for someone special.

ORIGAMI

Origami, or paper folding, is a creative way of turning a piece of paper into something else like an animal, hat, or cup. Scientists and artists also use origami to create models and art. You can buy special origami paper that is easy to fold and holds its shape well, but you can also use any paper you already have at home.

ORIGAMI CROWN

Make a crown that is the perfect size and color for you.

WHAT YOU'LL NEED

Paper

Tape (optional)

1   Start with a square piece of paper and fold it in half. Then fold it in half again. Unfold it all the way. Your paper will be divided into fourths.

2   Fold down the top right corner to the centerline and then fold the top left corner to the centerline.

3   Take the bottom edge and fold it up to touch the bottom of the triangles and crease it.

4   Take that rectangle and fold it up again so that it is above the base of the triangles.

CONTINUED →

STEP 1

STEP 2

STEPS 3 & 4

ORIGAMI CROWN *CONTINUED*

5 Repeat steps 1 through 4 seven more times. You now have eight different pieces.

6 Slide the rectangles into each other to connect each piece. Connect them into a circular crown shape. Remove pieces to make the crown smaller, or make more pieces for a larger size. Use small pieces of tape to hold the pieces in place if necessary.

STEP 5

STEP 6

THE HISTORY OF ORIGAMI

Origami is the art of paper folding. It started
in China when paper was invented and then
became popular in Japan in the seventeenth
century. Paper was a luxury back then and not
many people had it, so origami was usually
used to make things for good luck or for
celebrations like weddings.

ORIGAMI CORNER BOOKMARK

Never lose your page again with this cool corner bookmark.

WHAT YOU'LL NEED

Paper

Marker or pencil
(optional)

1 Start with a square piece of paper and rotate it so it looks like a diamond.

2 Take the bottom point and fold it up so it meets the top point. Now you will have a triangle with a crease at the bottom.

3 Take the bottom right corner and fold it up to meet the top point. Take the bottom left corner and fold it up to meet the top point. Those two folds are next to each other in the middle.

4 Open those folds so your paper is triangle-shaped again.

5 Take one of the layers of the top point and fold it down to the bottom in the center.

6 Lift up the right corner, fold it up toward the middle, and tuck it inside.

7 Take the left corner, fold it up toward the middle, and tuck it inside.

8 You can also add details like eyes and a mouth to turn it into a bookmark character.

9 The bookmark is ready to slide onto the corner of a page in your favorite book.

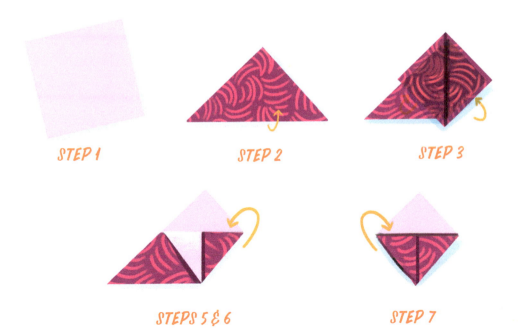

STEP 1   STEP 2   STEP 3

STEPS 5 & 6   STEP 7

ORIGAMI CUP

Follow these steps to make a cup you can use to hold a snack or sip some water.

WHAT YOU'LL NEED

Paper

1 Start with a square piece of paper and rotate it so it is in a diamond shape.

2 Fold the bottom point up to the top point and crease. Now you have a triangle shape with the crease at the bottom.

3 Take the top points and pull them down to the left corner. Crease and then unfold it.

4 Now you have a new diagonal line across the triangle shape. Take the right corner and fold it up to where the diagonal line starts. Crease.

5 Pull the left corner across, just like you did with the right corner.

6 You have two loose triangles at the very top of your shape. Fold down one triangle to the middle and crease. Flip over the cup and fold down the other triangle to the middle and crease.

7 The cup is ready. Gently squeeze the sides to open the paper into a cup shape.

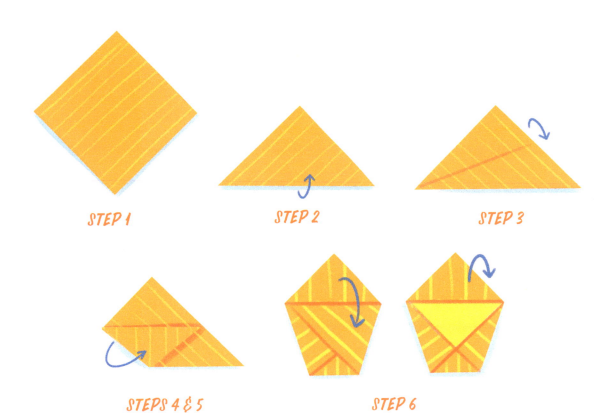

STEP 1

STEP 2

STEP 3

STEPS 4 & 5

STEP 6

ADVENTURE GIRL CHALLENGE

Share your talents by teaching someone else how to get creative with origami.

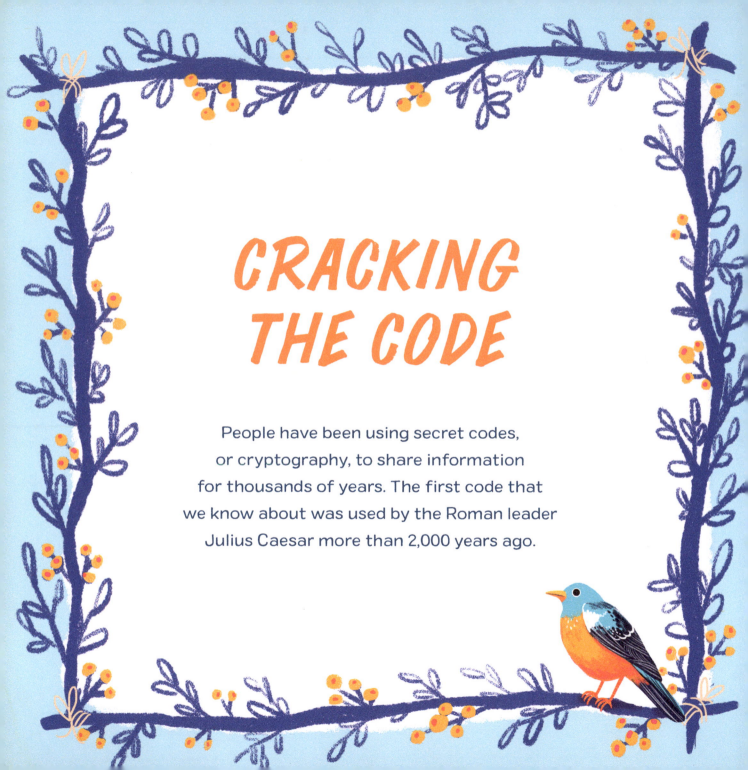

CRACKING THE CODE

People have been using secret codes, or cryptography, to share information for thousands of years. The first code that we know about was used by the Roman leader Julius Caesar more than 2,000 years ago.

INVISIBLE INK

Make your own invisible ink and use it to write secret messages. The only people who will be able to read your words are people who know the special way to make them appear.

WHAT YOU'LL NEED

2 tablespoons baking soda

1 cup water

Cotton swabs

Paper

Juice

1 Mix the baking soda and water. This will be your invisible ink.

2 Dip a cotton swab into the invisible ink mixture and write a message on your paper. You will be able to see what you are writing because of the moisture on the paper.

3 Let the paper dry completely.

4 To make the invisible ink reappear, dip a cotton swab in a small cup of juice (any kind will work) and rub it over your paper. Your message will appear. Hold it up to the window for an even cooler view of the message.

SECRET CODES

Codes are a fun and clever way for Adventure Girls to share secrets. Use these codes to write letters to your friends or to keep what you write in your journal private.

HALF REVERSED ALPHABET

With the Half Reversed Alphabet, each letter stands for the letter opposite of it on the chart. For example, A stands for N and N stands for A. J stands for W and W stands for J. To write the word CAT you would write PNG.

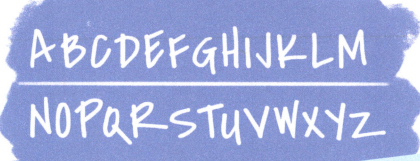

ADVENTURE GIRL CHALLENGE

Make up your own secret code and teach a friend how to use it. Write messages to each other using your code.

PIGPEN

The Pigpen code has been around for hundreds of years. With the Pigpen code, you replace each letter with the symbol from the chart.

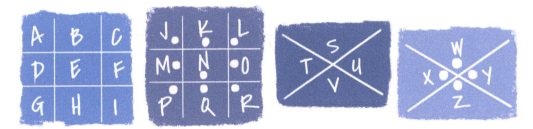

The letter E has a box around it.

To write the word DOG you use these symbols:

EVERY OTHER LETTER

This code requires that you only read every other letter to form a message. Use the first letter, skip a letter, use a letter, skip a letter, etc. For example, AHDRVUEPNKTHULRAEOGPIMRCLWS says Adventure Girls.

MAKE A DECODER WHEEL

Make a spinning decoder wheel with a secret combination to write and read messages.

WHAT YOU'LL NEED

2 paper plates

Scissors

Brad

Ruler

Pencil

Markers

1   Trace and cut out two different sized circles from paper plates.

2   Put the smaller circle in the middle of the larger circle and attach them to each other in the center with a brad.

3   Use a ruler and pencil to divide both circles into 32 sections. Put the ruler on the circles and draw a straight line starting at the brad in the center and going all the way to the edge of the largest circle. Continue making straight lines until you have 32 sections.

4   Number each space of the smaller circle from 1 to 32.

5   Fill the sections of the larger circle with letters from A to Z. There will be extra spaces to add different shapes, like a star, smiley face, or triangle. You can put those shapes anywhere you'd like mixed in among the letters.

6 Use markers to add color or decorations to your decoder wheel.

7 Decide on a secret combination to set the decoder wheel to before you are writing or reading your code. For example, turn the circles until the star and the 10 line up. Your code would be Star 10 and the wheel would need to show this before you make a code or read a code. Don't forget to mix up the decoder wheel when you are done using it so nobody else can decode your messages.

BOOKWORMS

Whether they like books that make them laugh, make them cry, make them think, or make them sleep with the lights on, Adventure Girls love stories! Write your own with these fun writing challenges.

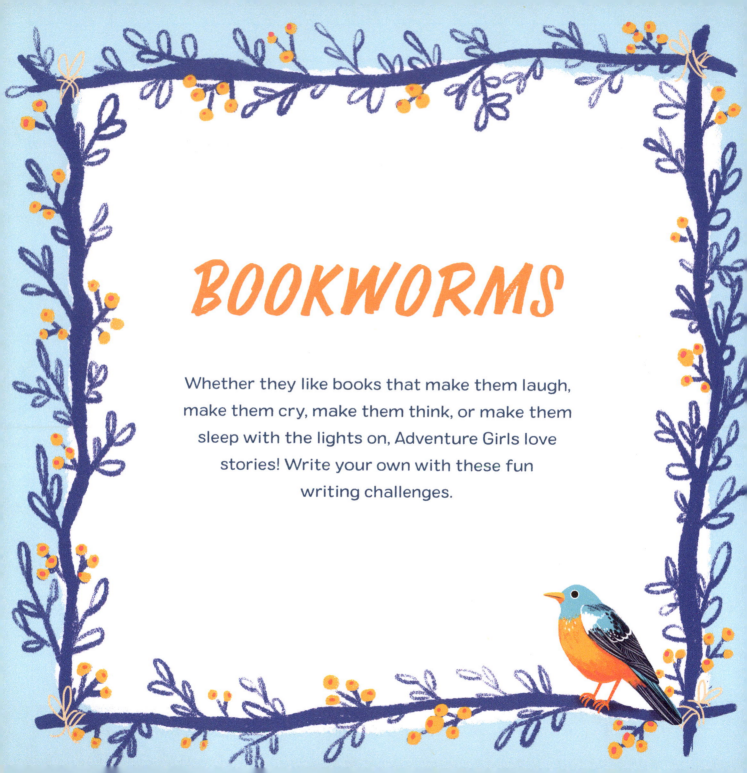

PICK A BOOK, ANY BOOK

Take a book from your shelf, flip to a random page, and read the first sentence. Use that sentence as the first line in a story of your own.

WRITE BACKWARD

Think of a sentence that sounds like the last line of a story, such as, "They never saw each other again." Then come up with a first line as different from the ending as possible, such as, "Nick and Arabella were inseparable." Now you have the frame of a story. Start writing to fill it in!

WRITE TOGETHER

Write a story with a friend by taking turns adding paragraphs. When you write a paragraph, fold the paper over to cover the whole paragraph, except the last sentence. Your friend will read your last sentence, add their own paragraph, and fold the paper to cover their whole paragraph, except the last sentence. Continue taking turns until you fill up a page or two.

ADVENTURE GIRL CHALLENGE

Make your own book. Write several short stories or even a short novel and bind them together (use the Nature Journal directions on page 34).

PLAYING IN TREES

Trees are a valuable resource and are important to our environment. They are homes for animals, insects, and birds. They create oxygen for us to breathe. And climbing or swinging from their branches can be so much fun!

MAKE A ROPE SWING

Nothing feels more like sun, fun, and freedom than swinging from a tree. Hold on tight!

WHAT YOU'LL NEED

Tree

Thick rope, 10 to 12 feet long

1 Find a strong tree with a low sturdy branch.

2 Throw one end of the rope up over the branch.

3 Securely knot the rope to the branch, with the help of a parent or another adult.

4 Ask an adult to help you test the rope by slowly putting weight on it. Once it is secure, grab on and swing!

WATCH LEAVES BREATHE

Trees and their leaves are living. They take in carbon dioxide that we breathe out and then turn it into oxygen. Watch a leaf release its oxygen with this simple experiment.

WHAT YOU'LL NEED

Clear glass bowl

Water

Leaf

Rock

1 Fill a clear glass bowl halfway with water.

2 Pick a leaf from a tree or bush.

3 Put the leaf in the water and put a small rock on top of it so the leaf is completely underwater.

4 Leave the bowl next to a sunny window.

5 After a couple of hours, check on the leaf. The small bubbles you see are the oxygen that the leaf is releasing.

STEP 1

STEPS 2 & 3

STEPS 4 & 5

HOW LEAVES MAKE FOOD

Leaves use sun, water, and nutrients from the soil to make food for their plant. Try this experiment to see how a leaf gets water.

WHAT YOU'LL NEED

Clear glass cup

Water

Red food coloring

Scissors

1 Fill a clear glass cup about halfway with water.

2 Put a few drops of red food coloring into the water.

3 Pick a leaf from a tree. Make sure the stem of the leaf is still attached.

4 Cut a small amount off of the bottom of the leaf's stem.

5 Put the stem of the leaf in the red water.

6 Observe the leaf every day. By the third day you should see where the red water has traveled to the veins of the leaf, just like water and nutrients would travel there.

ADVENTURE GIRL CHALLENGE

Go out and climb a tree! Look for a sturdy tree, one that has a low, strong branch that you can reach easily. Grab the branch and swing your leg up and into the spot of the tree where the branch and the trunk meet. Reach for a nearby branch and keep climbing!

PRACTICE KINDNESS

No matter how old you are, you can change
the world. With acts of kindness, big and small,
you can make a difference. For one week, write
down all the acts of kindness that you do.
Set a goal of three acts of kindness per day.
Remember, small things make a big difference.

MAKE A NEW FRIEND

Being friendly is one way to show kindness. Look for someone who doesn't have a partner or is sitting alone at lunch and invite them to join you. Saying hello or even just smiling will help you meet someone new and spread kindness.

VOLUNTEER

Volunteering your time and energy to help your community is another way to practice kindness. There are many people who need help. One way you can help is to fill bags with food, water, socks, or blankets and keep them in the car. When you see someone that needs help, you are prepared and can give them a bag of supplies.

Whether it is at church, school, or in your city, helping others spreads joy. Ask a local organization how you can help or volunteer your time.

DO SOMETHING SMALL

Small acts of kindness make a big difference. Try holding a door open for someone, picking up litter if you see it on the ground, or offering to help a family member or neighbor. Although all of these actions seem small, they add up to make a big difference.

10 MORE ADVENTUROUS WOMEN THROUGH HISTORY

MELISSA ARNOT

(1983–present) Melissa Arnot is a mountain climber who has climbed to the top of Mount Everest six times. She teaches wilderness classes and guides people on mountain hikes.

BESSIE COLEMAN

(1892–1926) Bessie Coleman was a pilot and stunt performer at a time when there were few opportunities for women to fly. She was also the first African-American woman with a pilot's license.

LOUISE BOYD

(1887–1972) Louise Boyd photographed and explored the Arctic Ocean. She was the first woman to fly over the North Pole.

SYLVIA EARLE

(1935–present) Sylvia Earle is a marine biologist and oceanographer who has explored oceans around the world. She now teaches others how to care for our oceans.

SARAH GOODE

(1855–1905) Sarah Goode was an inventor who invented a folding cabinet bed that could also be a desk for people living in small apartments.

DANICA PATRICK

(1982–present) Danica Patrick is a racecar driver and was the first woman to win the IndyCar Championship.

SUE HENDRICKSON

(1949–present) Sue Hendrickson is a paleontologist who discovered the most complete Tyrannosaurus rex skeleton, which was named Sue in her honor.

SACAGAWEA

(1788–1812) Sacagawea was a Native American guide who helped Lewis and Clark survive their famous expedition across the western United States from 1804 to 1806.

MARIA MITCHELL

(1818–1889) Maria Mitchell was the first woman astronomer in the United States. She discovered a telescopic comet.

VERA RUBIN

(1928–2016) Vera Rubin was a well-known astronomer who studied galaxies and made new scientific discoveries.

ABOUT THE AUTHOR

 **NICOLE DUGGAN** is a passionate educator with a master's degree and many years of experience in early childhood education. Staying home with her children led to the start of the blog *The Activity Mom*, where she empowers parents to connect with their children through learning. Join her at Activity-Mom.com for more inspiration.